THE GRI
MONOLO
FROM THE HUMA

ERIC KRAUS is the co-founder of Smith and Kraus, Inc.

JON JORY is the Producing Director of the Actors Theatre of Louisville.

i

Other Books for Actors from Smith and Kraus

The Best Men's Stage Monologues of 1990
    edited by Jocelyn Beard

The Best Women's Stage Monologues of 1990
    edited by Jocelyn Beard

Street Talk: Character Monologues for Actors
    by Glenn Alterman

Great Scenes for Young Actors from the Stage
    Craig Slaight and Jack Sharrar, Editors

The Best Stage Scenes for Men from the 1980's
    edited by Jocelyn A. Beard and Kristin Graham

The Best Stage Scenes for Women from the 1980's
    edited by Jocelyn A. Beard and Kristin Graham

One Hundred Men's Stage Monologues from the 1980's
    edited by Jocelyn A. Beard

One Hundred Women's Stage Monologues from the 1980's
    edited by Jocelyn A. Beard

THE GREAT
MONOLOGUES
FROM THE HUMANA FESTIVAL

DISCARDED

Edited by
Eric Kraus

SK
A Smith and Kraus Book

A Smith and Kraus Book
Published by Smith and Kraus, Inc.

Cover and text design by Jeannette Champagne

Manufactured in the United States of America

First Edition: November 1991
10 9 8 7 6 5 4 3 2 1

Publisher's Cataloging in Publication
(Prepared by Quality Books Inc.)

The great monologues from the Humana Festival/Eric H. Kraus.
p. cm.
Includes bibliographical references.
ISBN 1-880399-00-8

1. Monologues. 2. Acting. I. Kraus, Eric H.
PN4307.M6   808.8245

                                    91-66286

Smith and Kraus, Inc.
Main Street, P.O. Box 10, Newbury, Vermont 05051
(802) 866-5423

ACKNOWLEDGMENTS

Many thanks to the playwrights and their agents. We would also like to thank Michael Dixon and Jon Jory at the Actors Theatre of Louisville for their help and support with this project.

CONTENTS

CONTENTS

CONTENTS

INTRODUCTION

Usually it all comes down to one speech anyway. Somewhere there's a moment in the dialogue where the emotional center of the character or the play is revealed. These are moments the audience remembers. They bronze recollection like baby shoes. How many times have we heard, "You know, the play that has the speech about riding on a shoeshine and a smile."

The monologue is, of course, not merely an end in itself, but an art form that has seduced great playwrights from the beginning. It has often been the cream of the playwright's talent and can, in two minutes, evoke a world. The best, like good plays themselves, have a beginning, a middle, an end, an obstacle, an objective, a theme, an arc, and something in the character that changes before our eyes.

When the job's on the line for an actor, what's wanted is not just an expression, or explanation. Actors want the coiled spring of the words to explode them into concentration and feeling. The monologue, in that sense, plays with the actor or actress, not just through him or her.

So this collection of monologues from the Humana Festival of New American Plays is really an explosive group of energy sources for contemporary drama. They're also a kind of cultural history writ small, a miniature of our nation and our relationships. Bottled hearts as twere. Telegrams from the eighties and early nineties. Each a pandora's box for the play they were taken from. Each a distillation and powerful release.

Come and get 'em. They're hot.

—Jon Jory
Producing Director
Actors Theatre of Louisville

THE GREAT
MONOLOGUES
FROM THE HUMANA FESTIVAL

THE GIN GAME
by D.L. Coburn
A retirement home - Present - Weller Martin (70's)

Weller talks to his "girlfriend," Fonsia, about an experience of
old age which recently befell him.

WELLER: Sometimes I'll be sitting in my room...or even out
here...and everything will take on a dreamlike quality; people, the
room, everything...like it wasn't really happening. At first I could
snap out of it almost immediately. But then, a couple of times, it hit
me and I couldn't shake it. This feeling of sheer terror came over
me. God, I didn't know what to do. I'd sit there panic stricken, for
no reason at all. People around me would go about their business.
I don't think they even knew I was having a problem. And then it
would pass.

THE GIN GAME
by D.L. Coburn
A retirement home - Present - Weller Martin (70's)

Weller loves to play gin rummy. He lives in a retirement home. He has taught the game to a recent arrival, Fonsia Dorsey, but has been unable to defeat her even one time. Rage and frustration is gradually overcoming him. He prepares to deal a new hand to Fonsia.

WELLER: I'll worry about the doctors. You just play your cards and play them right. *(He puts the cards down and looks up at FONSIA.)* Fonsia, I'm going to get to the bottom of this. No. We're going to get to the bottom of this because you're going to help me. What we're going to do is...we're going to find out exactly what force is at work here. There's a reason that you constantly draw precisely the card you need—and you do, come hell or high water—and I'm going to find out what that force is. *(He deals.)* One, one. Two, two. Three, three. Four, four. Five, five. Six, six. Seven, seven. Eight, eight. Nine, nine. Ten, ten. Eleven. *(They pick up their cards. FONSIA looks at her hand, closes it, and puts it down on the table.)*

GETTING OUT
by Marsha Norman
Southern prison - Present - Arlie (20's)

Arlie, who is in prison for murder, talks to a pillow in her cell as if it were the baby which was taken away from her and placed in a foster home.

ARLIE: *(In the cell, holding a pillow and singing)* Rock-a-bye baby, in the tree top, when the wind blows, the cradle will...*(Not remembering)*...cradle will...*(Now talking)* What you gonna be when you grow up, pretty boy baby? You gonna be a doctor? You gonna give people medicine and take out they...no, don't be no doctor...be...be a preacher...Sayin' Our Father who is in heaven... heaven, that's where people go when they dies, when doctors can't save 'em or somebody kills 'em 'fore they even git a chance to...no, don't be no preacher neither...be...go to school and learn good *(Tone begins to change)* so you kin...make everybody else feel so stupid all the time. Best thing you to be is stay a baby 'cause nobody beats up on babies or puts them...*(Much more quiet)* That ain't true, baby. People is mean to babies, so you stay right here with me so nobody kin git you an' make you cry an' they lay one finger on you *(Hostile)* an' I'll beat the screamin' shit right out of 'em. They even blow on you an' I'll kill 'em.

3

LONE STAR
by James McLure
Texas - Present - Roy (late 20's)

Roy is drunk on a Friday night outside Angel's bar. He tells
about early experiences in his beloved pink convertible.

ROY: In the spring of nineteen hundred and sixty one I took Edith
Ellen Hyde out in that car a mine. Took her parkin' out to
Thompson's road. That was the night I looked up her dress. Up
until then I had no idea what life was all about. *(Pause.)* We kissed
and kissed till we got half way good at it. Then she took off her
shirt. *(Pause.)* That was the first nipple I'd had in my mouth since
Mom's. But nipples are like bicycles: once you learn you never
forget how. Finally we got the windows all steamed up, and I
couldn't wait. Got the car to smell like the smell of a woman and
I just had to see it. Edith Ellen didn't want me to see it. Said it
was bad enough me touchin' it without wantin' to look at it. She
even tried to scare me. Said it looked God awful. But she couldn't
talk me out of it. I was a man with a mission. So I scooted over
and scrunched down under the steerin' column like this and she lifted
up her skirt and I lit a match like that. And I looked at the damn
thing. *(Pause.)* And y'know, y'wonder what the first explorer felt.
The first explorer that climbed over that hill and saw—stretched out
before him, in all its God glory—the Grand Canyon. Well that's
what I felt like when Edith Ellen Hyde lifted her skirt and said,
"here it is," I looked, and it was AWE INSPIRING. I felt like
Adam. I felt like the man who discovered the Grand Canyon.

CHOCOLATE CAKE
by Mary Gallagher
Massachusetts - Present - Annmarie (late 20's)

Annmarie, who is a compulsive eater and who periodically spends time away from her husband, meets Delia, who has a similar story, at a motel. Annmarie tells Delia about her sex life.

ANNMARIE: *(After a painful pause, she nods.)* He used to want to do it all the time. Before we were married, I mean... We started going together in high school. I had a crush on him for months, and then at a sock hop, this girl I knew dared me to ask him to dance, and I did. It was the only time I ever asked a boy to dance. I remember he had on a mohair sweater, pale green with a V-neck. He was chunky even then, and in all that mohair, he looked like a fuzzy lima bean. There were playing "Blue Velvet," you know, that real old Bobby Vinton song? We started dancing double-clutch, and he was sweating like crazy, and he had on all this English Leather...I never felt so warm and safe, you know, wrapped up in all that mohair, like in a cocoon or something... Ever since, it's just been Robbie. *(Slight pause; then.)* We waited to get married till we had two thousand dollars saved. Robbie didn't want to start with debts. So I said, "Okay, but we're not gonna do it till we get married." I made him wait. *(Appealing to Delia for the answer.)* Maybe it's my fault, maybe I wrecked it, making him wait like that. [DELIA: What? He couldn't get it up?]
ANNMARIE: I don't know. I don't know what it is. We did it on our honeymoon. But something wasn't right. He'd get upset and stop. And I'd be afraid to say, "What is it, what's the matter?" And then he just quit trying. I waited and waited...and finally a couple of times I tried to start it. But I felt funny about it, you know. I probably didn't do it right. He'd say, "Cut it out, Annie." One night when he said that, I started to cry. He said, "What's the matter, honey?" And I said, "There's something wrong, isn't there?

CHOCOLATE CAKE

I mean, we never do it." And Robbie said, "A lot of couples never do it. That's the best-kept secret. A lot of couples don't even like each other. But we love each other. We like doing things together and talking together and just holding each other close like this. So if we don't do it very often, we're still pretty lucky, you know?" So I said, "Yeah, I guess you're right."

[DELIA: Ha!]

ANNMARIE: Yeah...I can't help thinking, maybe it's because I've gotten fat. So I try to diet, you know, I really try! But it's like he doesn't want me to! I don't know what he wants! And I get to feel so lonely...and so empty...

[DELIA: Yes.]

ANNMARIE: I've never told that to a soul...I felt so ashamed. But maybe you can tell me. Do you think...I was afraid to ask Robbie about it, I know he'd get all upset, but...there must be some kind of counselors to go to... If I tell Robbie everything, how much it hurts me that we don't make love...maybe he'd go see somebody with me...and everything would change. Do you think that could work?

CHUG
by Ken Jenkins
Rural Indiana - Present - Chug (20's)

Chug tells why he likes his girlfriend Freda (and let go of Moo-Moo).

CHUG: I liked Freda because she made me *aware*. Yeah. She really made me aware of...my ears. She made me aware of my whole body, but...she really made me aware of "listening."
She would say to me, "Listen, Chug. Really listen. Just stop. Stop twitchin' around 'n makin' noise. Just stop. Stop thinkin'. Just listen."
(He listens.)
And I would. I would do it.
(He listens.)
I really got to like it.
(He listens.)
You know...you listen to something for a long time 'n you start to feel like you understand it. You start thinkin' that you know the story behind what you hear. Like...you listen to ocean waves, 'n you hear stories about fish, and ships, 'n sailors, 'n storms, 'n deep, secret places. You listen to them glass wind chimes?...wind might come all the way from China. Or another galaxy.
And music? Brahms. Bach. Beethoven.
'N...Bullfrogs.
(He crosses to the tape recorder and removes the Environments *cassette. He inserts a cassette of "Stone Flute" by Herbie Mann, but does not push the "play" button.)*
Bullfrogs.
(He opens another beer.)
See.
On the 4th of July...Independence Day...1976...Bicentennial. Myself, 'n Freda, 'n Moo-Moo were at a folk art festival and goat roast down in northern Mississippi. Lots of good people. Good

7

CHUG

vibes. Lots of resonance. Well...we ate some roasted...goat...drank a little wine...were kinda laid back into the scene. Home made music and dandelion wine. Not too bad.

Not too shabby.

Well...long about sunset some of us were layin' around on a grassy slope near a little pond. Tellin' lies. Smokin' native grasses. Watchin' dragonflys. When Moo-Moo started moooooin'. Real low. Mooooo...moooooooo. 'N he kept it up...moooo...until he had everybody's attention. Moooooooo. Then he quit.

It was *quiet*. I mean it was real quiet.

Then...we all heard the bullfrogs.

They'd probably been singin' right along and we didn't notice.

But, when we all shut up...we could hear 'em.

And...we all got in to it.

It was a real experience.

We all sat there listenin' to the bullfrogs sing for an *hour* or more. Just listenin'.

'N the Freda turns to me 'n says, "Bullfrogs, Chug. It's bullfrogs."

'N I says, "It sure is."

'N she says, "This is the most resonant thing I've ever heard."

'N I says, "Very resonant."

"Fantastic rhythm!"

"Harmonious."

"There is only one mind here...and it has many voices."

"You said it."

"Chug. Chug," she says, "Chug...we have a lot to learn."

NOTHING IMMEDIATE
by Shirley Lauro
Iowa - Present - Edna Bloodwell (middle-aged)

Due to a blizzard, Sandra Warsaw Stein, a Columbia University
instructor has become stranded at the Lucky 6 Motel. Edna, a
bitter and judgmental proprietor of the motel, decides to lecture
politics to Sandra.

EDNA: *(Beginning to step toward SANDRA.)* You were very
"Politically Active." For Kennedy. Weren't you? *(She continues
to come closer.)* Weren't you? That's exactly what you meant by
"Before!" Marched yourself on down there to Washington, didn't
you? Threw beer bottles and cigarette butts on the White House
lawn? Ran, doped up, naked in front of the statue of Mr. Lincoln
from Illinois. Burnt up buildings! Draft cards! You and your Dr.
Alan Stein, the psy-chi-atrist! That is exactly what you mean by
"Active"! Ain't it? *(She is very close, SANDRA slides along couch
to other end to get away.)* Ain't it?
[SANDRA: We...we were part of the Movement...yes...a lot of
people were... *(She is at end, can't move farther.)*]
EDNA: And tellin' lies and gittin' lyin' articles in them newspapers
a yours about Mr. Richard M. Nixon, bless his soul to heaven, who
ended that war and kept all you Jews and Arabs quiet and outa
everybody's hair when he was President! That was a part a your
"Active Movement" too, wasn't it? All them newspapers and TV
stations all you people got yourselves hold of out there! To spread
lies about that beautiful God fearin' Christian man whose family
come from right here in this state! With that pretty wife of his had
a stroke on account a them lies you told. And them two pretty little
girls. Broke their hearts in two about their sweet Daddy. That was
your Movement out there in New York City! Wasn't it? Huh?
*(She comes as if to grab SANDRA. SANDRA now gets off sofa and
begins backing herself toward door leading to motel rooms.)*

9

CEMETERY MAN
by **Ken Jenkins**
Cemetery - Present - Cemetery Man (65)

Cemetery Man, the grave digger, is reminiscing about his career.

CEMETERY MAN: Two brothers by the name of Johnson came out here and told me to dig a grave for their cousin. Said he'd got shot accidentally. Said that they'd have the preaching and all that at the house, and that they'd bring the Body out here the day after tomorrow. They handed me a 5 dollar bill and went on their way.

Well. I dug the grave, The day came. Towards evening here they came. Just the two brothers and a pine box.

They said, "Where's the hole?"

I said, "Right here."

And then, without so much as a "farewell brother" they plunked the pine box down in the hole and turned to go.

I said, "No family? No preacher?"

They said, "We done took care of all that. Just fill it in."

They gave me another 5 dollar bill and went off down the Hill. "Well," I thought, "This is a downright peculiar. But, it ain't no concern of mine what kind of ceremony, or lack of one, that anybody has. That ain't none of my business."

Well...about the time I'd throwed the third or fourth shovel of dirt down in the grave...I commenced to hear a low, moaning sound coming from inside the coffin.

Now, I don't scare easy, but that sound made the hair stand up on the back of my neck.

I thought, "I better take a look."

So, I got my pry bar...and, just as I was reaching down into the grave...the lid on the coffin busts open and out crawls this hairy, bloody man!

I almost wet my pants.

Well, he started moanin' louder and jumpin' around like he was

THE CEMETERY MAN

a going to get a hold of me...so, I reared back with my pry bar to let him have it. I meant to do it, too!

Dead man or not...I didn't want him putting his hands on me!

Well. All of a sudden he stood stock still and pointed his bloody finger at me and said, "I must be in Hell! You must be the Devil! Lord God Almighty! I never knew the Devil had a face like that!"

And then he took off running down the Hill.

And then I saw that I'd been played for the fool.

See? A little ways down the Hill I saw the "dead" man meet up with the Johnson brothers...and they all three fell down on the ground and rolled around...they were laughing so hard. I just stood there while they pointed their fingers at me and held their sides...they were laughing so hard.

They were rowdy boys. Do anything for a joke. For a story. They got me pretty good. I got to admit it. Got me pretty good.

They're layin' together over there on the North side.

Where their Mom and Dad can keep an eye on 'em.

Not that it'll do much good. Never did.

EXTREMITIES
by William Mastrosimone
Suburban house - Present - Raul (30's)

Raul has forcibly entered Marjorie's house and is in the process
of abusing and raping her.

RAUL: If you're nice! Be nice! *(removing the pillow)* You don't
want me to do it again, eh? *(shaking her head no)* Maybe you like
to get hurt, eh? *(Shaking her head no. Pause. He smothers her
again out of whim. She goes limp.)* Holy mother of god. A
freckle. I didn't know you had freckles. I love freckles. I want to
kiss 'em all. Give 'em names and kiss 'em all goodnight. Yeah.
The first time I saw you I knew it was gonna be beautiful, but I
didn't think this beautiful. I didn't think anything could be this
beautiful... Not anything... Beautiful. *(He kisses her gently.)*
Don't make your lips tight. They always make their lips tight. Do
it nice. No. They're still tight. Kiss me nice. Yes. Yes. Nice.
Smile. Smile! Nicer! How ya doin? Answer me!

EXTREMITIES
by William Mastrosimone
Suburban house - Present - Raul (30's)

Raul, in the process of abusing and raping Marjorie, has had the
tables turned on him. He is now blindfolded and bound and is
appealing to Marjorie, now his captor, for release.

RAUL: You there? My eyes burn! I need a doctor! You there?
I'm hurt bad! Help me! You there? Where are you? *(MARJORIE
dials the phone.)* Call the cops, pussy! You can't prove a fuckin
thing! *(Realizing the phone is dead, she drops it and watches RAUL
buck.)* Why don't you fuckin answer me! You bitch! I'll kill ya!
Get the cops! They gotta let me go! *(MARJORIE runs up the
stairs.)* Your Honor, I goes out looking for work cause I got laid
off the car wash and I sees this farmhouse and goes t'ask if there
was any work cause I got three babies t'feed, and this crazy lady
goes and sprays me with this stuff, Your Honor. *(MARJORIE
rushes down the stairs holding her clothes in hand, opens the door,
but stops upon the mention of her name.)* Go on, Marjorie, go down
the road and stop a truck on the highway an tell 'em get the cops.
You got no bruises, no witnesses, no come up your snatch. You got
nothin, pussy. *(MARJORIE inadvertently lets the door slam.)* This
is a civilized fuckin country, pussy! You don't go around tyin up
innocent people, Marjorie!

EXTREMITIES
by William Mastrosimone
Suburban house - Present - Marjorie (20-30)

Marjorie has captured and bound Raul, who was in the process of abusing and raping her. She is now abusing him. Her roommate has returned home, and has accused Marjorie of becoming like Raul. Marjorie replies.

MARJORIE: Like him? I crave to be like him! No mind, no care, nothing human holding back the impulse to strike, tear, slash, and reduce him to splinters of bone! O God, make me more like him! Don't stare at me! Forgive me for surviving. Maybe you'd care more if you came home and tripped over my body and found animal waiting for you! What's going on here! Don't I count? What about me? Don't I count.

MY SISTER IN THIS HOUSE
by Wendy Kesselman
Lemas, France - 1933 - Lea (14-16)

Lea and her sister, Christine, are hired out as domestics by their mother. Lea has just begun a new job and speaks to Christine, who is also her figure of mother-love.

LEA: Dear Christine. When Maman left me here on Friday, I thought I would die. They didn't want to take me at first, but Maman told Madame Crespelle I was fifteen. Christine, I wish you could see what they eat. You can't imagine the desserts. The cook told me Madame's favorite dish is duck with cherries and Monsieur's, chicken with champagne. I'm hungry all the time. But it isn't as bad as I expected. I even have my own room. Do you think you could ask Madame Roussel to change your day off to Wednesday, like mine? *(She pauses.)* Today Madame Crespelle smiled at me. She was pleased with how the silver looked. I had been polishing it all morning. It was worth every minute for Madame's smile. When she smiles she looks just like Sister Veronica. *(A bell rings. LEA moves closer to CHRISTINE.)* Three days ago Maman came and took me away. She said I could earn money somewhere else. I was just getting used to the Crespelles, but I'm getting four more francs a month and Maman's promised to let me keep one of them. The Cottins have one daughter, Mademoiselle Sophie. Her birthday is next week. She's only two months older than me. She's so pretty. Her skin is like milk. And Christine, you should hear her play the piano. *(She pauses.)* Madame Cottin counts everything. Even the chocolates in the glass bowl. But I remember everything you taught me. And I think Madame will be pleased with me. *(She pauses.)* Every morning Madame Cotting examines my fingernails before I make the beds. Her things are so delicate. So many ruffles. So many buttons. You wouldn't believe how many buttons. It takes me two hours to iron one dress. And even then Madame isn't satisfied. *(She pauses.)* In this house I'm always afraid I'll do something wrong. Not like you, Christine. You never make mistakes. *(She pauses. Longingly.)* Oh Christine, if only Maman would place us together. *(A bell rings, almost interrupting LEA's last sentence. LEA goes down to her hands and knees and begins polishing the floor. CHRISTINE looks out.)*

CLARA'S PLAY
by John Olive
Montana - August 1915 - Sverre Lundgrensen (40's)

Sverre Lundgrensen is a Norwegian immigrant who has found work fixing up Clara O'Keefe's farm. Having realized that Clara is not only crazy but also poor, he has just returned from town where he has gotten drunk and into trouble.

SVERRE: *(from offstage, quite drunk)* Clara! Clara! Clara! *(Enters staggering.)* Hey, Miss Clara, you see this Norway fool? I think you are very proud of me tonight. *(Does an elaborate pantomime.)* Kraut farmer, stripe overall, smelling like hog slop. He say, "Hey. Swede-boy. You telling us now 'bout crazy woman 'cross lake. Got woman for boss, eh? Now going to poor farm. How about you give us hot gossip? Boy. Dumb Swede." Bam! Kraut flying across room. Bam! Kraut have many friends in saloon, very unhappy with Sverre. Bam! Bung! *(Whirls around, stumbles, falls to his knees, queasy.)* Uff da. *(A pause, then he goes to the pump, gets a drink of water.)* Aaaggghhh... *(Splashes water on his face.)* Sheriff coming tomorrow, taking me to clinker. Take us both to clinker. You try to kill sheriff, I try to kill Kraut. Big trouble in Maple Lake. *(Stands, in his fake accent.)* Goin' to yail, by yumpin' yiminy. *(SVERRE goes to CLARA, looks at her. A beat. Then SVERRE quickly turns away, stands downstage, breathing shallowly.)* Hey, Miss Clara, you get wet in the rain? Very nice, eh? Boom! Rain! Now stars. And cool. So beautiful. I am telling you, Norway never like this. Never so black. Three o'clock in Norway, sun rising. Never dark like this. *(Slaps his arm.)* Mosquitoes. *(laughs)* Farm alive, eh? Full with mosquitoes. I am never going home. *(Beat. Turns, looks at CLARA, then again turns away.)* This is a very beautiful farm, Miss Clara...beautiful farm, Miss Clara. Lake. Stars. New orchard. *(pauses)* Three years since I am leaving home, Miss Clara. I am very...tired. *(Another, longer pause: SVERRE sits on the ground, leaning against the porch, near CLARA, looking out over the lake.)* Oh, Clara.

A DIFFERENT MOON
by Ara Watson
Arkansas - 1959 - Sarah Johnson (35)

Sarah, an unsophisticated farm woman, surprises Jean, a
sophisticated young (17) lady, with a cleverly presented ghost
story.

SARAH: It was one night last summer and I was sitting in our
living room at home all by myself 'cause everybody else had gone
visiting into town and I didn't want to. I just thought they'd be back
early like they always do, but it kept getting later and later and it
was one of those pitch black, real dark nights—the moon was mostly
behind the clouds. So, I was sitting there and I started getting a
little bit scared 'cause I don't ever like to be in that old creaky house
at night by myself. See, we don't have any neighbors for miles and
miles and—oh, yeah, there'd been these murders out near there—ax
murders and they'd never even caught the person who did it
and—and right then I begin to hear this sound coming from out
front...wo-o-o-o-o...like wind in the pecan trees, but not, 'cause
there wasn't any wind—it was real still...wo-o-o-oo-o..
[JEAN: Sarah.]
SARAH: And, then, it stopped. Just like that. I could just hear
myself breathing is all. Dead quiet. And, then, it starts again only
louder...and it's closer...wo-o-o-o...and all of a sudden, I remember.
Oh, my lord, I forgot to lock the doors.
[JEAN: Oh, no.]
SARAH: And I know that whoever, whatever, it is can see me
'cause I'm sitting right in the light, so I ease over... *(And she eases
over to the lamp)* ...very, very, slowly, very carefully to the light
and I turn it out as fast as I can. *(She turns out the light, leaving the
room bathed in the light from outside, and stands for a moment.)*
Then I walk as quietly as I can to the front door and the sound is
getting closer and— *(Suddenly she stops and listens.)*
[JEAN: *(Small little voice.)* Sarah?]

A DIFFERENT MOON

SARAH: Sh-h. Do you hear that?

[JEAN: What?]

SARAH: *(She listens, trying to locate the direction of the sound—then quickly.)* Is the back door locked?

[JEAN: *(Quietly.)* I don't—]

SARAH: *(Quietly-urgently.)* Listen. Like...like someone dragging something heavy across the yard. *(She looks quickly toward the kitchen door, then back to the front door. Jean does the same.)* Oh, Jeannie, I can't tell— *(She looks quickly toward the kitchen door again and she holds very still, listening.)* It's at the back door.

[JEAN: Sarah.]

SARAH: Oh, my lord, it's in the house...

[JEAN: *(Tiny voice.)* No...]

SARAH: It's...it's coming in— It's coming— *(And at this point, Ruth enters through the kitchen door, making a noise as she does so. Jean immediately screams. Sarah laughs.)*

FULL HOOKUP
by Conrad Bishop and Elizabeth Fuller
Omaha - Present - Ric (late 20's)

Ric finds his wife Beth hiding in her mother's mobile home. He tells her that he knows about her indiscretion.

RIC: I came up those steps, I was gonna beat the shit out of you. I was.

Make you feel it.

And then I sat down. Changed the channel. And here we are.

I quit the job. *(Silence.)*

Cause I drove by.

And then I parked.

And then I sat and waited till he came out. *(Silence.)*

And hell, I had three pizzas, they were all stone cold.

So I dump'em in the trash and call up and quit.

But that's ok, cause he looked like he had a good time. *(Silence.)*

And when I went to a bar and I thought hell, why don't I write about it?

Write about something real.

Cause you can almost see it.

They're in bed there, and she opens up and starts doing her little act.

Hour and thirty-five minutes.

I could write about that. *(Silence.)*

But what's to write?

Couple of people bouncing up and down, that doesn't mean shit.

So it's ok, no sweat.

It doesn't mean shit.

FULL HOOKUP
by Conrad Bishop and Elizabeth Fuller
Omaha - 1980-1981 - Beth (25)

Beth is talking to her lover on the telephone. She is fearful of her husband finding out about the affair.

BETH: Hon...

Hon...

No hon.

No, he drove past and saw your car in the drive.

No, not today.

No, sure I liked it.

Sure I did.

No, I'm not sorry we did it, sure I want to, but I can't today cause I can't take the chance, he coulda stopped, what if he comes walking in...

No I can't. In the morning if I miss again they'll fire me, they docked me three days...

Anyway, I don't feel good, I'm kinda...sore, you know what I mean? Maybe we better lay off...

Hey, sure I did. Would I done what I did?

Dave, please, I'm scared.

Hey don't talk like that, you know I don't like that.

I don't like that word.

You know what word.

Now stop it, Dave, I'm gonna hang up...

No, shut up...

Shut up... *(She starts to cry. Listens, shaking her head, trying to protest. Abruptly strikes chair arm. Talks rapidly: flat tone.)*

Yeh ok.

Sure, you know damn well.

Come over early, one o'clock.

You're not gonna stay long.

Ok. *(Hangs up.)*

Oh you fuckers.

You fuckers.

You fuckers. *(Blackout. Lights, distant: Joellen.)*

21

FULL HOOKUP
by Conrad Bishop and Elizabeth Fuller
Omaha - 1980-1981 - Joellen (late 20's)

Office supervisor Joellen talks about Rosie, one of her office workers.

JOELLEN: Ok, I explained the supply invoices.
I requisitioned a new chair, she was having trouble with her back.
Listen to all her personal problems, and I've had it.
I think she's crazy.
You give in, she just finds a wedge and she shoves on in.
She complains about the coffee, she complains about her stomach, her back, and she's made the office miserable...
She has skills, but I think she's mentally disturbed.
Maybe it's family stuff, but you can't work with a crazy woman, and I think she's crazy.
I really do, I really think she's crazy.
I just don't want to know people like that.
I know they exist, but I just don't have the time.

FULL HOOKUP
by Conrad Bishop and Elizabeth Fuller
Omaha - 1980-1981 - Rosie (50's)

> Rosie's daughter has been murdered by her son-in-law Ric but
> she believes he is innocent. Rosie practices her testimony for
> the defense for Ric's upcoming trial.

ROSIE: Sure, he's my son-in-law, he's always been fine.
I thought very highly of him, he's going into electronics.
I could tell how upset he was, I knew he never did it,
  you can't fool a mother... *(Starts to break. Controls.)*
No, she was always in trouble.
She'd lie to me, and after she quit the church you knew
  she was doing stuff, stay out all hours.
That smile, that was a fake...
I'm telling the truth.
I was out at the dance, but I called Ric, I called him, and
  we talked on the phone, cause she was over to supper and
  he couldn't come over and I wanted to say hello...
I'm telling the truth.
She was running around with guys, I know that for a fact,
  maybe one of them was the one...
It's the God's truth.
We were going to the dance, and she told me there's this guy
  she's running around with, he was a dago, this dago, this...
He was this colored guy, this nigger from North Omaha,
  they're all over Omaha, and he told her he'd kill her...
That's the truth, I swear to God.
She was in college she's always sticking up for the niggers,
  and that's why she was in the trailer, cause this nigger
  was going to kill her.
I swear to God. I'm telling the truth.
She was always dirty like that.
She was a whore.

FULL HOOKUP

Beth was a whore.

A little pissyass whore. *(Starts to break. Controls. Les, holding receiver, shifts. Ric chews a stick of gum. She looks at album page.)*

Don't look at me, I'm telling the truth.

God's truth.

Try to fool me. You never look like that. Party dress.

That doesn't look like you ever looked.

There's no resemblance.

I'm not gonna keep that. *(Tears photo.)*

See the hate in your eyes.

Sure, all smiles.

It's a fake. *(Tears photo.)*

You got the look.

Sticking out your tits. *(Tears photo.)*

You're what's left. Leftovers. *(Tears photo.)*

Rip it out.

Clear out the weeds.

Plant some four-o-clocks. *(Tears photo.)*

New Year's.

You don't exist.

You don't exist, Bethie.

It's New Year's...

BARTOK AS DOG
by Patrick Tovatt
City - Present - McCormack (55)

Mrs. McCormack is interviewing a 35-year-old mainstream dropout, who wants to drop back in, for a night watchman's job. When she indicates "no," he complains about society's "vicious damn circle." She takes this personally and replies.

MCCORMACK: I'm *sick* and *tired* of being called a vicious damned circle! You're finally facing the consequences of a haphazard, self-indulgent life and because the nut's a little tough to crack you blame some vicious system! Well, I'm part of this circle. I'm proud of it and I can tell you how it goes in *my* part of the world. You're not gonna get this job...not because you didn't ask nicely enough. You've got a very good veneer there, for about five minutes...your materials are presentable enough. I suspect your girlfriend or somebody who has a job showed you how to organize it. You're healthy, you say you're smart, I'll even take your word for it. It's the *content*, the message here that causes the difficulty... This is a dismal history of self-indulgence and sloth. You can get away with this for a while...but this...you're 35 years old. Are you paying a life insurance plan? Silly question. Give me a good reason why any business would give you the opportunity, yet again, to walk away from responsibility *once again*, as soon as you've gotten the wherewithal to finance another damned adventure. And don't think for one damned minute I'm insensitive to your paranoia about discipline and routine...I've been doing this job, in this office for twenty three consecutive years, so I damn well know the price and the benefits of discipline and routine. You think I'm a drudge but I don't care because I'm not sponging and I'm not fighting self-disgust and don't tell me you're not because I can smell it. *(Pause, McCormack shuffles papers.)*
[PARSONS: You know this may be one of those situations... where...]

25

BARTOK AS DOG

MCCORMACK: And I *know* right down to the bedrock bottom of my mean stony old soul, that there's *not a thing* I can do for you.

[PARSONS: I was thinking maybe I oughta go...]

MCCORMACK: You shoulda thought of all this years ago...

[PARSONS: Mrs. McPherson...]

MCCORMACK: Mrs. McCormack. Now I'm going out to get a cup of coffee.

[PARSONS: *(He starts to laugh.)* Okay.]

MCCORMACK: I want you gone before I get back...I suggest you go somewhere and quietly reflect on your situation.

[PARSONS: *(He is laughing steadily now.)* Okay.]

MCCORMACK: There are those who set a steady course and those who wander aimlessly... If I hired you, I'd be sabotaging my company, and I wouldn't do that for *anybody!* There's nothing worth stealing in that desk. *(She goes.)*

IN A NORTHERN LANDSCAPE
by Timothy Mason
Minnesota - 1926 - Emma Bredahl (16)

Emma has been persuaded by her mother to try on her wedding dress. Her brother, Samuel and his friend, Anders have been teasing her and have left for a college party. She is trying to remove the dress and is speaking angrily.

EMMA: Oh, woe unto you, Samuel! Woe unto you! Scribe. Pharisee. Hypocrite! "Run along, now, Emma!" Oh, woe unto you, you... *(Whispered undertone.)* ...bastard! *(Pulling with difficulty at her garments.)* Disgusting old dress! Try to tie me up, will you? Chop! Off with his hands! "She's just a child, she has *moods!*" Oh, I'll give you such a mood, Sam... *Your* moods change with the wind, for goodness sake. "Oh, yes, you look good in it, Emma." Woe unto you, Anders Thorson! Sissy! "Little girls *like* to dress up." Well, I'll dress up in my skin from now on—that's what I'll wear. *(In her anger, she is having difficulty getting the dress off.)* God *damn it to hell! (The gown and foundation garments cling around her ankles. She kicks at them futilely, and then sinks to her knees, half crying with frustration.)* Dress myself in skin and air and live alone in the earth and never be lonely...me and the rabbits... *(Samuel re-enters through the screen door, and starts up the stairs.)* The dogs live out there... But at least with them you're never tempted to trust them, you're never going to love one of them by mistake, they just are and you never have to do anything but hate them. Just one thing to hate and one thing to love. *(Kicking halfheartedly, wearily, at the dress.)* God damn this old dress. *(Samuel enters second level, R.)*

A TANTALIZING
by William Mastrosimone
Metropolis, USA - Present - Ambrose (60ish)

Ambrose is a derelict with style.   He is invited into the
apartment of a single young woman, Dafne, whose heart goes
out to him. He is arrogant and argumentative in response to her
kindness. In a burst of anger she throws a bowl of soup at him.
She then apologizes and hands him a towel. Ambrose responds.

AMBROSE: *(snatching the towel, hurling it at her)* Gloaters!
Flies! You flies! How you love to see an eagle fall out of the sky!
and tumble in the street! You flies! You love the smell of carrion!
You flies! Come study the grimace! Behold the spectacle! Come
witness the agony! Flies! Come land your petty eyes on me and
feed your insatiable little stomachs! Flies! Know that once these
savaged hands could take disaster and turn it to legal tender! Failed
stock, damaged commodities, flooded land, bought for nothing and
made to turn a pretty penny, while you flies, disgusting, buzzing,
shit-eating flies, earn dollars by the hour! Where other men saw
calamity, these eyes, blessed with vision, saw a ripe sweet fig
dangling just out of reach, teasing me, nodding in the breeze,
overripe, teasingly.   I saw all the possibilities, all, all the
permutations and combinations, all, and one would lead to two
would proliferate to six, to a dozen; one call would lead to another
to another... [*(He picks up his phone.)* What'd you do to my
phone?]
[DAFNE: I haven't touched it.]
[AMBROSE: It's dead.]
[DAFNE: It was dead.]
[AMBROSE: I made calls.]
[DAFNE: Wire's cut.]
[AMBROSE: Who cut it?]
[DAFNE: It was cut.]
[AMBROSE: But I made calls!]

A TANTALIZING

[DAFNE: No.]

AMBROSE: *(He is seized by the sudden realization of his condition. He gasps, back to the wall, and slides down to the floor, covers his face with his hands.)* Take it all, flies! Shoes and coat and watch and eyes and fingers and my will! And when I have nothing, nothing, nothing, when I fall down a man in the noontime street, lay flat on the walk, would it be enough for you if I rise up a roach and scurry under your sink? Would that be enough?

A TANTALIZING
by William Mastrosimone
Metropolis, USA - Present - Ambrose (60ish)

Ambrose, a derelict, has been welcomed by a young woman, Dafne, into her apartment. She has fed him and is attempting to clean him up when she discovers he is bleeding from a dog bite. She asks why the dog bit him.

AMBROSE: Because nature gave it teeth. If it had wings, it would've flown away. Soupbone. Left for me by the chef. He remembers when I used to pick up the tab. Leaves the soupbone out back. In newspaper. Rolled up. Sometimes a roll. Sometimes with butter. Sometimes a few potato skins. But always the bone. Soupbone. For the marrow. Ever eat marrow? Utterly nectareous. Nature endowed only the canine and the most astute epicurian palate the distinguished receptors to appreciate this most piquant delicacy. And I found this mongrel with one ear,—Dapple I call him, —savoring my supper. I watched it jaw the bone sideways and crack it, its hot tongue folded sideways running with saliva lapping out the marrow. And I brained it.

A TANTALIZING
by William Mastrosimone
Metropolis, USA - Present - Dafne (late 20's)

Dafne has taken a derelict, Ambrose, into her apartment. He angrily bemoans his lot to her. His talk stirs memories of Dafne's father, who met with a tragic and untimely demise. Dafne speaks to Ambrose about her father.

DAFNE: Sir? *(pause)* Sir? *(sitting on piano stool)* My father froze to death out in the street. He suffered a stroke some months before and it left him not so responsible for himself. If you took an eye off of him, he'd wander out. You'd find him out on the street asking strangers for pocket change, or stealing apples at the corner market, or looking through a garbage can. It was quite embarrassing for the family. Such a comedown for him, from what he was before. *(pause)* Dad was a restorer. A historian with a hammer. When I was younger he would take me sometimes. I'd hang onto his long scarf and walk in the wake of his pipe smoke. Cherry blend. Funny: I catch a wiff of that now and suddenly he's there. He'd take me to a cold ramshackle house where hinges screech and a rat would run for cover, where the roof leaked and the stairs buckled and floors warped, some landmark building. And grave men would be waiting there, and they'd make a big fuss over me, and asked Dad if he would restore this disaster back to the original condition. And Dad would puff on his pipe and give a hard look. His eyes could see under decades of abuse and neglect; penetrate slapdash coats of cheap garish paint; strip away and sandpaper the dereliction down to the run in the grain of the wood. And he'd say, "Yup," and then do more than he promised. *(pause)* It was lunchtime when a police officer saw a passerby tripping over what he thought was a vagrant on the sidewalk. He nudged the vagrant with his billyclub. *(pause)* They say freezing is the kindest death. First you tremble, then you get numb, then you curl up like a baby in a crib, and sleep.

THE VALUE OF NAMES
by Jeffrey Sweet
Hollywood Hills - Present - Benny Silverman (70)

Benny's daughter, an aspiring actress, has just told him that she
landed a part in a play which requires her to take her top off.
Benny reacts negatively. She defends the plays seriousness.
Benny replies.

BENNY: In your mind it may be about vulnerability. Maybe in the
playwright's mind. In the audience's mind it will be about tits. The
women out there will be thinking, "Gee, I couldn't do that. Well,
maybe I could do that. But how many Margaruitas would it take?"
Or maybe they'll be comparing. Are yours bigger than theirs, are
theirs rosier than yours. Meanwhile, the guys in the audience will
be thinking... Well, you *know* what they'll be thinking. And their
wives will know what they're thinking. And the women'll look at
their husbands like they're saying, "Yeah, and what are you gawking
at?" And the guys will go, "Hey, I'm not gawking." And the
women'll go, "Oh, yeah, right." And the guys will go, "Hey, but
it's OK: this isn't tits, this is art. I'm having a catharsis here.
Swear to God. And, yes, honey, I really do like yours better."
You're up there acting your heart out, in the meantime, they've
forgotten your character's name.

A WEEKEND NEAR MADISON
by Kathleen Tolan
Wisconsin - 1979 - Jim (30's)

> Jim reminisces to his sister-in-law, Doe, of a weekend with
> Nessa, his former girlfriend who has since chosen lesbianism as
> a result of her feminist philosophy.

JIM: That afternoon David retrieved me from my little cell and we
walked down the road to Chad's. It was this incredible day—bright
and windy and it smelled like snow—in fact they were forecasting
the first storm, so Chad and David and I got into this kind of frenzy
to beat the snow.
[DOE: Uh-huh.]
JIM: We were splitting and stacking and yelling and cursing and
telling stories, and then the work itself—the physical labor—together
with being out in that day—kind of overtook us. And we just kept
going, lifting and splitting and lifting and splitting, in silence. Just
our breath and the chopping and throwing and the sounds of the
woods... And when we'd done half of it, we hopped into the truck
and drove the rest up to our place and went at it there... And I was
panting and aching and soaked with sweat—I had no idea where the
strength was coming from to lift the ax. At one point I straightened
up and just stood there. The light was fading, the sky was a pale
yellow, cut with a thin string of charcoal clouds. A patch of the
yard was washed with a golden light from the kitchen window. I
looked up, and you and Nessa were standing there, looking out at us.
And I waved. And you both waved. And, I felt this fullness...I've
never felt so full...of life...as I did at that moment. *(pause)* And I
felt like a man. A man. In some deep, ancient sense. *(pause)* I
don't know. I mean, if I were honest, I guess I'd say that's all I
really want. That kind of romantic, traditional thing. I mean, it did
feel like we were continuing something...the men outside, splitting
wood for the long winter, the women in the kitchen cooking dinner.
I mean, I mean, everything else seems so insignificant when I think
of that moment.

A WEEKEND NEAR MADISON
by Kathleen Tolan
Wisconsin - 1979 - Nessa (30's)

Nessa, a lesbian who has recently "come out" defends her
position to an old friend, David.

NESSA: So what if there are things that aren't, like, "tasteful."
And any movement is gonna attract fucked up people as well as
strong, healthy, intelligent people, and some who would've been
sympathetic are turned off. Well so fucking what. They'll be part
of the second wave. I mean, you know this, David, any movement
is going to alienate people who are too lazy to look at the main
intentions of the movement. And I'll tell you something. I came out
because I was sick and tired of being a goddamn "sympathizer."
(pause) It's the only way. I really believe that. Women have been
oppressed for so long that nothing is going to change if we keep
sleeping with our oppressors. I'm sorry, but it's true. Okay, just
look at sex. Men fuck you, and the only way, this is true, think
about it, the only way to really get off is to submit, I mean there has
to be an element of that, of letting go, d'you know, to have it work.
So if you're letting go with the people who are keeping you down—.
And if it's one of those rare cases where the guy isn't an asshole,
and he really cares about who you are, it's even harder. Because if
the guy is that sensitive he's gotta be really fucked up. *(beat)* Think
about it. We have all been so programmed in so many ways to think
of the woman as serving the man. The only way to change that is
for women to return to the source. To each other. It's the only
way.

COURTSHIP
by Horton Foote
Harrison, Texas - 1917 - Laura (17)

Laura and her older (20) sister Elizabeth have strict, overbearing
parents. Laura reveals some of her fears to Elizabeth.

LAURA: I wish to heaven I didn't. Everything bad that happens to
a girl I begin to worry it will happen to me. All night I've been
worrying. Part of the time I've been worrying that I'd end an old
maid like Aunt Sarah, and part of the time I worry that I'll fall in
love with someone like Syd and defy Papa and run off with him and
then realize I made a mistake and part of the time I worry... *(A
pause.)* that what happened to Sibyl Thomas will happen to me
and... *(A pause.)* could what happened to Sibyl Thomas ever
happen to you? I don't mean the dying part. I know we all have to
die. I mean the other part...having a baby before she was married.
How do you think it happened to her? Do you think he loved her?
Do you think it was the only time she did? You know... *(A pause.)*
Old, common, Anna Landry said in the girls room at school, she did
it whenever she wanted to, with whomever she wanted to and
nothing ever happened to her. And if it did she would get rid of it.
How do women do that?

EXECUTION OF JUSTICE
by Emily Mann
San Francisco - 1978 - Douglas Schmidt (30's-40's)

Douglas Schmidt, Defense Attorney for Dan White who is on
trial for the murder of San Francisco Mayor Moscone and
Supervisor Harvey Milk, gives his closing statements to the
Court.

SCHMIDT: I'm nervous. I'm very nervous. I sure hope I say all
the right things. I can't marshal words the way Mr. Norman can—
but—I believe strongly in things. Lord God! I don't say to you to
forgive Dan White. I don't say to you to just let Dan White walk
out of here a free man.   He is guilty.   But, the degree of
responsibility is the issue here. The state of mind is the issue here.
It's not who was killed; it's why. It's not who killed them; but why.
The state of mind is the issue here.

Lord God! The pressures.
Nobody can say that the things that happened to him days
or weeks preceding wouldn't make a reasonable and ordinary man
at least mad,
angry in some way.

Surely—surely, that had to have arisen, not to kill,
not to kill, just to be mad, to act irrationally,
because if you kill, when you are angry, or under the
  heat of passion,
if you kill, then the law will punish you,
and you will be punished by God—
God will punish you,
but the law will also punish you.

Heat of passion fogs judgement, makes one act irrationally,
in the very least,
and my God,

36

EXECUTION OF JUSTICE

that is what happened at the very least.

Forget about the mental illness,
forget about all the rest of the factors
that came into play at the same time;
Surely he acted irrationally, impulsively—out of
   some passion.

Now...you will recall at the close of the prosecution's case,
it was suggested to you this was a calm, cool, deliberating,
terrible terrible person
that had committed two crimes like these,
and these are terrible crimes,
and that he was emotionally stable at that time
and there wasn't anything wrong with him.

He didn't have any diminished capacity.
Then we played these tapes he made directly after
he turned himself in at Northern Station.

My God,
that was not a person that was calm and collected and cool
and able to weigh things out.
It just wasn't.

The tape just totally fogged me up the first time I
   heard it.
It was a man that was, as Frank Falzon said, broken.
Shattered.
This was not the Dan White that everybody had
   known.

Something happened to him and he snapped.
That's the word I used in my opening statement.

EXECUTION OF JUSTICE

Something snapped here.

The pot had boiled over here,
and people that boil over in that fashion,
they tell the truth.

Have the tape played again, if you can't remember what
   was said.
He said in no uncertain terms,

"My God,
why did I do these things?
What made me do this?
How on earth could I have done this?
I didn't intend to hurt anybody.
My God,
what happened to me?
Why?"

Play the tape.
If everybody says the tape is truthful, play the tape.
I'd agree it's truthful.

With regard to the reloading and some of these little
discrepancies that appeared to come up.
I am not even sure of the discrepancies,
but if there were discrepancies,
listen to it in context.
"Where did you reload?"
"I reloaded in my office, I think."
"And then did you leave the Mayor's office?"
"Yes, then I left the Mayor's office.:

That doesn't mean anything to me at all.

EXECUTION OF JUSTICE

It doesn't mean anything to me at all.
And I don't care where the reloading took place!

But listen to the tape.
It says in no uncertain terms,
"I didn't intend to hurt anybody.
I didn't intend to do this.
Why do we do things?"

I don't know.
It was a man despreately trying to grab at something...

"What happened to me?
How could I have done this?"

If the District Attorney concedes that what is
on the tape is truthful,
and I believe that's the insinuation we have here,
then, by golly
there is voluntary manslaughter,
nothing more and nothing less. I say this to you in all honesty.
And if you have any doubts our law tells you,
you have to judge in favor of Dan White.

Now, I don't know what more I can say.
He's got to be punished
and he will be punished.
He's going to have to live with this for the rest of his
    life.
His child will live with it
and his family will live with it
and God will punish him
and the law will punish him,
and they will punish him severely.

39

EXECUTION OF JUSTICE

And this is the type of case where, I suppose
I don't think Mr. Norman will do it
but you can make up a picture of a dead man
or two of them for that matter
and you can have them around and say
somebody is going to pay for this,
and somebody *is* going to pay for this.
But it's not an emotional type thing.
I get emotional about it
but *you* can't
because you have to be objective about the facts.

But please, please
Just justice.
That's all.
Just justice here.

(SCHMIDT appears to break for a moment.)

Now I get one argument.
I have made it.
And I just hope that—
I just hope that you'll come to the same
  conclusion
that I have come to,
and thank you for listening me.

HUSBANDRY
by Patrick Tovatt
Kentucky farm - Present - Harry (37)

Harry, who is visiting his parents at their farm with his wife
Bev, realizes that his parents can't "make it" as farmers any
longer because of the "bureaucratic system." He discusses the
unfairness of this situation with Bev.

HARRY: Hey...I'm doin' my level best. But...aww, I know what
you mean, darlin', I won't help goin' around with a long face,
*but...but...*I am absolutely pissed off about...and feeling shit
worthless about a whole lot of stuff. And it's the same old
maddening thing...if enough people, et cetera, et cetera... But now
it's my father and it's...and I mean the farming, not the arthritis.
And part of my problem is, I'm confused cause I thought I *knew*
something about the farm situation...you know? *(pause)* The reality
is...you've got my father, a model American entrepreneur. Owns
his own place of business, risks his own money...doin' a good job,
just makin' enough to get along, but he keeps doin' it! A real solid
citizen if there ever was one. An asset to the community. Goin'
along makin' *food*. And he's *so* good at makin' it that they've come
up with a whole system for keeping him from makin' *too much*...
whatever that means. What does over-production mean in a world
where, say, a third of the people are near starving? *(pause)* And
now, he's caught in a lethal cost and interest spiral and more and
more politics and bullshit...speculators...regulators...all of the
bureaucratic crap that I deal with every day magnified a million
times...only it's brokers and middlemen and processors and shippers
and buyers and the agri-business hotshots...*all* of 'em conspiring to
use the government to keep the price of his goods low... You can't
tell me there's no demand...people are *dying of starvation!* And he's
got nothing to say. He's gotta sell and take what he can get...so
he's basically gonna go under because...nobody gives a damn about
the one really important link in the whole chain from the dirt to the

HUSBANDRY

gravy stain, you know on the silk tie of your average senator.
Nobody seems to understand that the ones who tend the soil...who live on it, and listen to it and try to keep it strong because it *feeds* them...and care about it's mysteries...and there are mysteries, by God, not yet penetrated by Purdue University...It's people like my folks that keep these communities...that keep these communities...communities. Him and all his kith and kin... *(pause)*

HUSBANDRY
by Patrick Tovatt
Kentucky farm - Present - Harry (37)

Harry, who has come to visit his folks at their farm, realizes that
they cannot "make it" as farmers without his help. He tries to
convince his wife, Bev, that they should become farmers in
order to save the farm.

HARRY: Bullshit! You seem to think the resolution to this whole
issue is up to you and Ma! The situation has several other aspects
for me... *(pause)* I'm not sure I want to be the one who breaks this
chain of...of stewardship...better yet, of husbandry, that all my
people have been a part of...it's the family business, Beverly. Only
we never thought of it in those terms because it was the folk's farm,
he farmed it. Well, now he...now he needs what keeps these places
family farms...he needs his son.

Pa put it to me plain and simple...as a business proposition, but
first and *foremost* he said, was decide if it's a *good* thing for the
people...you and me and Sadie and Ian...And I'm just trying to find
a way to get you to consider it from my place...I can't just kiss off
this whole situation and say you settle it folks, ain't no business of
mine, cause it *is*. Maybe they shoulda had five sons, but that isn't
the way it worked out. So you've gotta allow me to treat this
seriously and not jump in my face everytime it comes up. We've
gotta *think* about it, at least. You and me...so let's stop
fighting...I've had enough hassle for one night...

HUSBANDRY
by Patrick Tovatt
A Kentucky farm - Present - Dee (55)

Dee, realizing that she and her husband may have to give up
their farm, discusses with her daughter-in-law, Bev, what will
become of the farm's contents.

DEE: Oh, those are the ones I have *up*. My mother passed me
down, oh my, fifty or so of the same vintage. She loved pictures.
They're all in this attic. You know, I was thinkin' the other day
these old houses and barns and sheds are crammed with old things.
Furniture with a leg missing and tools and odds and ends that don't
work anymore but you couldn't bear to throw away...and nice
things...my mother's photographs and, my land, Aunt Margaret's
dollies! And if we sell out, the junk traders will swarm over this
place like army bugs and by the time all this paraphernalia gets
divided up...because where am I going to put it all, in a house in
town? By the time it winds up in antique shops from here to China,
it'll be worth more than the land. *(pause)* The *vanity*...the
arrogance...to prize the worn out, useless old junk and sacrifice the
heart and the meaning and all the real value...cause you know, it's
the bond between the people and the earth that is the farm...the land
is just the land.

LEMONS
by Kent Broadhurst
South - Present - Desenelle (55)

Desenelle is the super-secretary/office manager who runs the show at Beuchel Goodee Motors (car dealership). Here she returns from lunch.

DESENELLE: O Buddy precious, I'm sorry I'm late. We had a anniversary luncheon a the "Dozen an' One Club" and O my Lord. It was Belle-Mai's turn to plan it. I'm gonna see to it she don't get to do it anymore. That's why I'm late. She got us reservations at some damn Mexican/Soul Food place. Had this exotic male dancer...well, a *stripper's* what he was.
[BUD: Sounds like the girls had a hot lunch.]
DESENELLE: I was so embarrassed I could hardly eat. I was right on the end a the booth. He kept wrigglin' up to me an' pullin' it out. Right there where they serve the *food*. That don't turn me on...had this *huge* red...sequin sombrero. *(Bud and Wade are nearly on the floor.)* SURE! Sit there an' laugh. I don't know who'd wanna see anything he's got. They was all gigglin'n gaspin'n pourin' down cantelope coladas'n hollerin' for Marguerita. I thought, now what the hell's *she* gonna come out in. I consider myself as broadminded as the next person, but some things just stick in my craw. I was ridin' with Marmalada and 'course Elmer's Glue couldn't keep her knees together and she wasn't about to leave, so 'course that made me late for my appointment to get my hair done.

THE OCTETTE BRIDGE CLUB
by P.J. Barry
Rhode Island - 1944 - Connie (56)

Connie, whose bad back is giving her great trouble, tells her sister about her confrontation with a neighbor during their monthly bridge game.

CONNIE: The other day I was out in the backyard hanging my corset out on the line to air out...and the little boy, Wayne, from next door came over. He asked me why I walked like a gorilla. I told him I had back trouble. He said his grandmother had back trouble but she didn't walk like a gorilla. I told him his grandmother walked like a penguin. He said he thought so, too...and did we laugh!...and off he went. About an hour later, I went out back to get my corset *off* the line, reached up, lost my balance and flopped back on my behind. I sat there, I couldn't get up, don't ask me why...like being paralyzed, I just couldn't get up for the life of me. It started to drizzle. I had the corset in my hand so I put it over my head for protection and shouted: "Help! Help!"...waited...hummed songs...prayed for my boys. Next thing you know the corset's being lifted by Wayne's mother. "Mrs. Emerson, did you tell Wayne that his grandmother walks like a penguin?" I said: "Yes, I did." She said she thought it was a terrible thing to say to a boy his age, and I said he said I walked like a gorilla and she said: "You do!"...honest. And I said: "I walk like a gorilla because it pains me to waddle like a penguin. Now would you please help me to my feet and give me back my gosh darn corset!"

THE OCTETTE BRIDGE CLUB
by P.J. Barry
Rhode Island - 1944 - Martha (64)

Martha, a widow in failing health, reveals some of her
frustrations to her sister during their monthly bridge game.

MARTHA: A few years ago I was shopping in Jericho,
Christmastime. I saw a man and a woman ahead of me in the street.
They were holding hands. I remember thinking: Look at them, at
their age, holding hands, behaving like children. And the couple
stopped, and turned to look in a store window. You were the
couple, Nora, you and Larry. I didn't approach you, turned and
hurried back to my car...got in behind the wheel...didn't move,
couldn't, couldn't start the motor, just sat and began to shake, angry
with Michael for dying and leaving me a widow with four daughters
to raise. I'd leaned on the horn. Somebody knocked on the
window. I rolled it down. A man with a handlebar moustache like
Michael's, asked me if anything was wrong. I said, "Yes" and he
asked, "What?" I told him none of his business and I spit right in
his face. *(pause)* I was so ashamed. I'd never done anything so
terrible in my life.

THE OCTETTE BRIDGE CLUB
by P.J. Barry
Rhode Island - 1944 - Betsy (47)

Betsy, who has recently returned from a lengthy stay in an asylum, tells her sisters the raw truth during their monthly bridge game.

BETSY: *(her courage growing)* I remember our third anniversary...ten years ago...here. That was the night the trouble started for me. Connie gave me a ride home, and I went inside, paid Mary Lou for babysitting, got my scissors from my sewing basket and I cut up the kitchen curtains I'd just made. And for...well, the next ten years...Doctor Carroll would call my...misbehaviors the flu...or nerves...and I'd be in bed for a week or two. Once I remember smashing all my Norataki China...Ann came over and helped me clean it up, and the next day I went to that psychiatrist who had such bad teeth and he gave me those pills that made me so groggy all the time. But every other Friday...the Octette Bridge Club was always something I looked forward to...safe. Oh, all of you seemed to think I was stupid, but—
[NORA: No.]
BETSY: I had the chance here to prove that I wasn't! I could win! I became something, a good bridge player...my claim to fame and fortune. *(pause)* I don't know why I did what I did. *(pause)* It was a beautiful day; and I was cleaning our room. When I finished I took Dan's pants and jackets and went out in the backyard and had a bonfire, and when everything was burned I went back inside and went into the bathroom and slashed my wrists.
[ANN: Don't.]
[MARTHA: You weren't yourself.]
BETSY: Dan had to commit me...he didn't have much choice. But I wanted to go, I think I wanted to go years before. I needed help. *(pause; attempting to override her tears)* Why didn't you come to see me? Oh, you sent gifts and cards and flowers...but not one of you came to see me. My sisters. *(pause)* That hurt so much.

THE ROOT OF CHAOS
by Douglas Soderberg
Centralia, PA - Present - Joe Cernikowski (40)

> Centralia has fallen victim to a huge underground mine fire
> which is gradually destroying the town above it and the people
> in it by fire or noxious gases. Joe has just lost his wife Wilma,
> daughter Doublemint, and son Skeeter. He confronts his
> solitude and fears.

JOE: I suppose you think that's funny, too. What's that supposed
to be, anyway? A stroke, or something? *(Pause.)* Skeeter?
Skeets? Son? *(Pause.)* Boy, that's rich. That's a hot one. You're
just a baby. A *stroke?!* What a corker! Perfect! Hysterical!
While I'm on the subject of really great laughs I've had in the past
hour, what about your mother getting fried in the basement? And
your sister getting struck down by lightning like that. Now that was
really funny. Of course, I shouldn't have been too surprised.
And...and my own mom and dad—I haven't thought about this in six
years—my own mom and dad in that supermarket explosion. That
was truly a riot. When that happened, I wanted to lay down and
laugh so hard. Till I had tears in my eyes. You know what I mean?
And I only had one brother, but he was born dead. That made me
an only child. *(Pause.)* Son? Are you really gone? *(He moves
away.)* Go ahead, then! Take off! Leave! See if I care! You
stupid, stupid, stupid! All of you!! *(Stopping.)* This means I...this
means I'm alone. *(Beat.)* Except for in-laws. *(Singing:)*
While we seek mirth and beauty
And music light and gay,
There are frail forms fainting at the door.
Though their voices are silent
Their pleading looks will say,
"O, Hard Times,
Come again no more!"
(Propping Skeeter's body on a chair at the table.) They say we're

THE ROOT OF CHAOS

individually always alone. Always, no matter what. But now...now I'm afraid. *(A series of three soft knocks is heard on the wooden porch door.)* Who's there? *(No answer.)* Pete? *(The three knocks are repeated.)* Pete, is that you? *(No answer.)* Oh...shit God. Skeeter! Skeeter, what did you mean about "plain old fear?" *(Knocks.)* Your sister said she was afraid to grow up like Mommy. That was just before— *(Knocks.)* And your mom. She was afraid I'd leave her. *(Louder knocks.)* What about you? What was it you—? *(Yet louder knocks.)* That's right. You were afraid there might not be a heaven or a— *(Three very loud knocks; he whispers:)* That's for me. *(The knocking becomes a relentless tattoo.)* No! I didn't mean it!! A family!! One lousy little family! Big deal! They were all scared of their own shadows, anyway! Alone? So what! Go away! *(He takes the theodolite and props it under the door handle. The knocking is now augmented—magnified and echoed.)* Leave me alone! Never mind what I said! I'm not really!! I'M NOT!! I'M NOT AFRAID!!

THE AMERICAN CENTURY
by Murphy Guyer
Small Town, USA - 1945 - Man (mid-20's)

Tom is just home from the war. He has just kissed his wife
Margaret and tells her of his optimism.

MAN: Margaret from here on out it's going to be nothing but the
best. I know it's hard to believe, but it's true... You know, when
we were driving through those small towns in France, I don't know,
you should've seen it. The streets were jammed with people.
Hanging from the street lamps. Leaning out the windows. And they
were all cheering, and screaming, and waving American flags. And
the women were holding up their kids for us to kiss. And this one
kid grabbed me and held me around the neck, and I looked into his
eyes and, I don't know. I don't know how to explain it. I just felt
that somehow it had all been worth it. It's a new world Margaret...
It's a whole new ballgame. That's what I felt when that kid hugged
me. I felt like anything was possible. Like there wasn't anything
we couldn't do, anything we couldn't have, once we put our minds
to it. And it's all out there. Just waiting for us to grab it. A life
more wonderful than we ever dreamed was possible... We made it
Margaret. We're home.

TWO MASTERS
by Frank Manley
Nursing home - Present - Ora Belle Ivey (50-60)

Ora Belle and Ruby are volunteers at a nursing home. Ora Belle
is a no-nonsense women who unwittingly finds herself sharing
an emotional experience with Ruby and Ray, a nursing home
patient.

ORA BELLE: Folks don't know what other folks thinking. That's
my observation. What other folks think's a mystery. You take my
momma. When she got like him—laying in bed waiting to die, ain't
no telling what she was thinking. She was laying there with her eyes
wide open staring at a spot on the ceiling. And I'd say, 'Momma,
momma, What're you thinking about, staring at that spot all day?
Don't you get tired?' Things like that, to cheer her up. I used to sit
there and watch her. It wasn't like him. Her mind was clear as a
bell, and she could talk if she wanted to. But she didn't want to.
Momma never did say a word, and I never did figure out what she
was thinking about, staring at the ceiling like that. She died with the
mystery still in her mouth before she could figure it out, what it
mean.
[RUBY: What mystery?]
ORA BELLE: What? Her whole life. *(as though speaking to
herself)* Like when you drown, you see your whole life flash before
you, like a great light, and there it is from beginning to end before
you slip under and die in the waves. After the funeral, I went up in
the room where she died, and I was alone. My momma and daddy
both were gone, and I was alone. *(RUBY gets up and walks toward
ORA BELLE.)* And the wind was blowing, and the house was
creaking, and I thought it was somebody coming up the stairs
creaking across the floor, and then it was like it came in the room
and I looked around and said, Who's there? But nobody answered.
And all of a sudden it was like some kind of blessing in there, and
I heard this voice, said, 'Ora Belle, you weren't able to help your

momma. She died staring at a spot on the ceiling, thinking something you don't even know what, like she was somewhere in some far-off land. But what about the rest of them? There's lots of others dying right now, this very minute. Old folks home's full of them, dying right and left. What about them?' And that's where I first got the idea of the errand of mercy. It's like somebody walked in the room and whispered it to me, except there wasn't nobody there. *(During this speech RUBY reaches out her hand and touches ORA BELLE as though to comfort her. ORA BELLE becomes aware of what is happening and pulls away abruptly, looking about her as though adjusting her eyes to an excess of light.)* Well I swear— *(as though surprised.)* Listen to that. Will you just listen to that, how I was talking? I swear, you all must be good company to get me to talking like that. I'm usually the quiet type. My momma used to say, 'You're the quiet type, Ora Belle. That's why you ain't married.' But it wasn't that. *(She falls silent again, glaring about her as though in anger.)*

21A
by Kevin Kling
Bus - Present - Ron Huber (Middle-aged)

The driver of the 21A bus between Minneapolis and St. Paul is
doing a crossword puzzle and telling about his route.

RON HUBER: Pardon my french but fuck the Twins that's how
'bout 'em. *(He goes back to the puzzle for a second.)* What am I,
a goddamn weatherman? I don't know it'll clear up. *(Goes back to
the puzzle. Suddenly he looks in the rear view mirror, jumps up and
runs to the back of the bus.)* Hey! Hey! Git away from there, you
kids. Git, I say. This ain't no goddamn toy. Git, I say. *(He
returns to his seat.)* Goddamn kids, they play on anything. I get a
new gas meter for the house and the next thing I know some
neighbor kid is rolling by on the old one. Made a goddamn gocart
outta it. Fifty bucks says I can leave something, anything in my
yard and the next day some neighbor kid is selling tickets to it. Shit
yeah, you can count on it. What, this route here? Oh, about two
years now. I've driven most of the others though, your two, your
three, four, seven, twelve, seventeen...I even drove the six for a
while. This 21 is a good route though. Ain't a day goes by I don't
say, "Shit, I never seen that before." It's a different kind of people,
see. Poor? I bet there ain't two bucks on this whole bus. Weary?
Some of these people have been through shit a cat wouldn't live
through. Crazy? No way. They're just as sane as you or me. Oh,
They're a little odd, most of them, you can bet on that. I don't
know how they keep from crackin' up. Me? I go up north fishing
with my brother-in-law, that would be Ray. Christ, we catch the
fish, really knock 'em down. Last year we limited out on Northern
and Walleye both. And the beauty of that country... Shit. We
were sitting there casting by the shore and I seen four deer come
down for a drink. I says, "Lookee there, Ray, I'd give fifty, no a
hundred bucks, for my deer rifle right now." See we got another
three months before the deer season so I just threw a rock. You

should meet this guy Ray though. He runs a chicken farm with my sister and two kids, that would be Joe and Bill. But these chickens, you don't eat 'em, see? Ray teaches 'em how to play Tic-Tac-Toe and then sells them to fairs. He makes pretty good money and they're good, too, boy. Shit, I tried all day, never could beat this one. But at these fairs they're in these little boxes, see? And pretty soon some of them chickens start to crack up. Well lookit, one minute they're a chicken on a farm and the next minute they're in a little box, trying to outwit a human. And when they lose just once, *(He makes a raspberry sound with his mouth.)* You might as well start mashing the potatoes. Fichu! Fishu! *(He writes on the crossword puzzle.)* It's a woman's triangular scarf. The way I see it we're all in some kind of box. Sometimes you find your way out, and sometimes you're stuck, like a chicken and then *(makes the raspberry)* it don't matter what bus you're on, a two, three, four...six, even. I gotta theory on people who thrive in boxes that will cost you a cinnamon triangle and a cup of coffee at the Super America. Hey, what is that crunchy shit in them cinnamon triangles, anyhow?... Oh, yeah? *(He stands up and puts out his cigarette.)* Say, lookit, folks. I'm going down to the Super America for a cup of coffee but don't worry, we'll start on time. *(He sets down the crossword and picks up his seat cushion.)* Goddamn kids.

HOW TO SAY GOODBYE
by Mary Gallagher
Cleveland - Present - Marty Staiger (25-33)

Marty is unambitious but very focused on Cover, his five month
old son. He talks about fatherhood.

MARTY: Yeah. He's just *right there*, you know? Look at him,
and he looks back. Smile, and he smiles. You just barely touch the
inside of his hand, he curls those little fingers up and hold on...he's
just *ready!* For the whole world!

[PHILLY: Yeah...]

MARTY: Scares me, you know? Wake up in a sweat sometimes,
dreaming how I'm gonna fuck him up.

[PHILLY: Maybe you won't.]

MARTY: Sure I will. I'm his father. *(Philly almost smiles. Beat;
then:)* But I figure, while he's still real little, I can't mess with his
head. And what I do for him is *real*. Change his diapers...feed
him...take him out to see the world! No one can say he doesn't
need all that! He does! And I can give it to him!...I wish I could
nurse him. *(Philly is thrown by this. Explaining:)* You know? To
give your kid the milk from your own breast...to know you were his
only source of life!...How could you feel like a washout? You
couldn't.

SOME THINGS YOU NEED TO KNOW
BEFORE THE WORLD ENDS
(A Final Evening With the Illuminati)
by Larry Larson and Levi Lee
A church - Present - Reverend Eddie (30-50's)

Reverend Eddie has nightmares that death has come for him.
He wakes and then the lights go out. He speaks:

REVEREND EDDIE: What happened to the lights? I'm not afraid
of the dark. I've had some wonderful times in the dark. *(Pause.)*
As if you didn't know. *(He strikes a match. Yells.)* YOU GOT
JOHN F. KENNEDY BUT YOU WON'T GET ME! *(Pause.
Smiles. Match goes out.)* AAAAUUUUUUUGGGGHHHHH! I
stepped on a foot! A bare foot! Someone else is here! I stepped on
a foot. *(Pause.)* And someone stepped on my foot! *(Pause.)*
Someone stepped on my foot and I stepped on someone else's foot
at the same time! *(Pause.)* They're both my feet. *(Pause.)* I'm
stepping on myself. I thought it was a big coincidence.
Synchronicity. *(Strikes another match.)* ...What? I heard that! I
heard that whispering! I hate that! If you can't speak up like a
man...then...something. I suppose you think your voices are too
small for the human ear! Well, *I* hear you! And I'm not afraid to
utter your unutterable name... *(He muffles it with his hands.)* The
Illuminati! *(Match goes out, burning him.)* Ooow! *(Pause.)* It's
probably just the wind. It's probably just my imagination. It's
probably the nerve gas. Oh Jesus, Lord and Master, its probably the
gas! They say this is what happens. You begin to hallucinate.
Everything begins to go dark. You begin to talk to yourself! You
begin to bleed from the nose and mouth...which I'm not, so it's not
nerve gas, thank God! *(He falls to his knees, strikes another match.)*
The Lord is my shepherd, and that's all I need. He is all green
pastures and quiet waters. He guides me in the paths of
righteousness for the sake of my good name. Even though I walk
through the valley of the shadow of death, I'm not afraid for the

SOME THINGS YOU NEED TO KNOW
BEFORE THE WORLD ENDS

Lord is with me and I am heavily armed. A table is prepared in the presence of my creditors. You annoint my head with oil. I feel good. I feel very, very, good. *(He is again in the dark.)* ...I know the rest of my days will be filled with goodness and mercy and love, and I will dwell... *(Match.)* ...Oh, Lord! See how my enemies have increased and how fiercely they hate me!... Whoever you are, and I know who you are. I do not pray out of fear! I've seen you lurking around in your clever disguises. I've seen you in your black suits and your black cadillacs and your frozen smiles, peeling blood money twenties and fifties from your obscene bankroll, paying off my enemies for work well done!!! Giving me night sweats and nightmares. Wet dreams and daydreams about my own mortality. Smiling about my predicament! Jumping to my conclusion and just generally hanging around just outside the perifery of my vision counting the vultures and puckering up for the kiss of DEATH! Well forget it! You don't scare me! You can put the lights out till doomsday and I won't crack! I love it! I hope the lights never come on! I hope it stays dark forever!!!!!

SOME THINGS YOU NEED TO KNOW
BEFORE THE WORLD ENDS
(A Final Evening With the Illuminati)
by Larry Larson and Levi Lee
A church - Present - Brother Lawrence (30-50's)

Brother Lawrence tells of a vision he has had.

BROTHER LAWRENCE: I had another one. It was a vision, not a dream. I know, because everything was so real. I was walking in the woods. It was winter, and very cold. I was afraid if I opened my mouth and took a deep breath that my teeth would crack and my mouth would freeze open. So I walked slowly and took little breaths. Finally, I came to big clearing. And...standing in the middle of this clearing was the Reverend Eddie. He was standing there, smiling, no hat and no gloves. And when I got closer to him, I saw he was smiling because he was happy. He wasn't sick like he is now, he was like he used to be. I was so glad to see him healthy again, and I could tell he was real glad to see me. He put his arms around me and hugged me, just like I was his son. And as he was hugging me, and laughing, all the pain in my body began to melt away. It started at the tips of my toes, like I was stepping into a warm bath. And the warmth spread all over my entire body, and all the pain was gone. Then the Reverend Eddie stopped hugging me, and stepped away. And he looked at me a long time like he was so proud of me. And then he said, "I'll race you to the trees" "One...two...three... go!" And we started running, and the more we ran, the more we laughed, until we were laughing so hard, we couldn't run another step. So we just fell down...and we laughed and talked until it got dark.

FUN
by Howard Korder
Roberson City - Present - Denny (15)

Denny and his pal Casper are cruising a local mall. Denny notices a Camaro in an inside exhibit and has a fantasy.

DENNY: Camaro's the best. *(Pause.)* Know what we could do?
[CASPER: What?]
DENNY: Get in that car, jump start her, tear ass off that platform all through this mall. Mow these fuckers down in their Hush Puppies.
[CASPER: Except the girls.]
DENNY: Crash it through the plate glass, man, bam through the GNC, bam through Hickory Farms—
[CASPER: Smoked *cheese*—]
DENNY: Bam through the Radio Shack, the fucking Waldenbooks—
[CASPER: Bam!]
DENNY: Then we ditch it in the fountain, right, we break some forty-fours outta Monty Wards, a couple of hunting knives, ammo, and we head upstairs, way up in the mall where no one ever goes, and there is this dude up there, okay, this fat asshole in a control room, all these screens and shit, and he runs the place, he plays all the muzak and makes the people walk around and smile and buy things only they don't even *know* it, and we shove him down on the counter and blow his fucking brains out.

ALONE AT THE BEACH
by Richard Dresser
The Hamptons - Present - Alex (mid-30's)

Alex, perceived as dull and reclusive by a group of
acquaintances with whom he has shared a beachhouse during the
summer, opens up for the first time and tells Chris, a female
roommate, how he came to discover computers.

ALEX: In a way I did. To save myself. *(beat)* What happened,
was, four years ago my brother, that is, my twin brother, we were
in business together. And he got sick and couldn't work all summer
and then in the fall he went into the hospital and I visited him every
single day after work and he was farther and farther gone until he
hardly knew me or my parents and still we thought he would
somehow recover. But of course he never did, and he died in early
December and watching him like that was like watching my own
death, we looked exactly alike and talked to each other without
words. When he died I knew that I had lost all my faith in God or
the future or anything at all. I got rid of our business and I moved
back in with my parents and there was really just nothing, I mean
every day was exactly like the last one and we hardly spoke to each
other. I lost track of time and stopped reading papers or listening to
music or doing anything at all. I just stayed in bed and after a while
I couldn't really tell when I was awake and when I was asleep and
what I had dreamed and what had actually happened. There were
times when I even thought that I was the one who had died and that
was what death was, living in this world where there was no time
and nothing happened, so I decided I had to do something in order
to be alive. I started fooling around with computers because the
information was real, it was not like believing in God or an afterlife
or something. A computer is really very simple. It makes a choice
between one thing and another, A and B. And it makes another
calculation on top of that. And another on top of that. And out of
all these simple choices, something much bigger and more complex

ALONE AT THE BEACH

is reached. I needed this information, these simple choices, because with more and more of them, built on top of one another, it was a way of reaching up and out of myself to get to a higher place where it was different from everyday life but I knew it was true. And I have this feeling about what I do that it is like climbing way up on this very fragile tower into the night-time sky and seeing the world from a different place and it is a way that I can maybe someday reach a point where I will have faith of my own again without using computers or anything else. That's what I would really like someday.

LLOYD'S PRAYER
by Kevin Kling
Middle America - Present - Bob (16-18)

Bob is a boy raised by racoons who has been adopted by human parents. He remembers his past.

BOB: Hello. Hello. Don't be afraid. I'm not. Are you new here? I said, are you new here? I'm not. This used to be my home but it seems different now...smaller. I don't seem to fit anymore. What's your name? What are you, then? *(Chatters.)* I wish I could speak to you but I've forgotten how. Sorry. I have been called many things in my life but I prefer Bob. I am an orphan. I could no more tell you my real father than the ingredients to a hot dog. I do remember my mother. I remember the night she became frozen and died. I remember snuggling next to her warm coat, my brothers and sisters crowding in to get at the milk but I was the biggest so I always got a spot. I remember her dark eyes. She taught me to always wash my food. She taught me to never trust a smile because that's right before something bites. I remember her on the side of the road. She saw the lights, became frozen and died. Lloyd says it happens all the time and she probably isn't in heaven because she didn't have a southern accent. Since I was the biggest, my siblings turned to me. I remember leading them to a house for food. The large metal cans full of food, the metal trap and the sound of my arm as it broke. I remember pulling to get free, pulling on the pain. I knew I was human. I knew when I saw the trap. I was not a racoon. I knew what I was doing. I was making a choice. I saw the trap, I saw the choice. I was human. I was human. I was human, I was trapped, and a man was running toward me with a gun. Lucky for me he was a doctor.

INCIDENT AT SAN BAJO
by Brad Korbesmeyer
San Bajo - Present - Paxton Spence (40's)

Paxton discusses how he happened to be saved when the drinking supply of San Bajo was poisoned.

PAXTON: It is really amazing to me that I survived. Here is this codger from God knows where and he's got this red liquid that he claims will make you live longer. Shades of the Old West and medicine shows, right? So you'd show him the nearest exit, the same exit stained with the footprints of freshly scrubbed pubescents who were two magazine subscriptions away from a trip to the Holy Land. I would ask him to leave. At least, I thought I would. I guess Joe did. *(Beat.)* But he wasn't selling the stuff. Not really. He didn't say it was the greatest invention since the tonenail clipper. He didn't list sixteen advantages his product has over the competitor's model. He simply said it would make me live longer. Boom. Take it or leave it. And against all odds, contrary to the cynicism it has taken me years to cultivate, I just as simply believed him. Coming from a childhood where my father was constantly selling his ideas, his inventions, his experience, his friendship, Maxlin's unadorned, unadulterated approach caught me off guard. I'm not saying I knew he was going to poison the town's goddamn drinking supply. I'm certainly not saying I knew this red liquid was the antidote. But I did sense I had to drink it. It was something, a feeling I picked up from him and embraced immediately. For a long time I thought that was odd, impossible really, that I would trust someone instantaneously. That faith in someone could be galvanized —flash frozen—in a moment's notice. Why not? I've spent years in relationships—at work, at home, at play—and never trusted the other party. Not really. So maybe trust has nothing to do with how long you work at it. Maybe it's more basic, sort of a connection certain people make with other certain people. When you recognize that connection, you can bet the mortgage on it, and you won't be disappointed.

STAINED GLASS
by William F. Buckley, Jr.
German village - 1952 - Erika Chadinoff (mid-20's)

Erika Chadinoff, a Soviet spy, criticizes Blackford Oakes, C.I.A. agent and would-be assassin of a West German political figure, for his government's hypocrisy and his own naivete.

ERIKA: You have no liver, Blackford Oakes. You fall for all that romancing of that dreamy prince about a unified Germany and you stop thinking. *(She rears her head in contempt.)* Add to all his other accomplishments, he has deballed Blackford Oakes. You talk with such excruciating delicacy about the function of the executioner. Only your government has just dotted all the i's and crossed all the t's to conduct an execution, spying, espionage, disinformation—nice going on the stories you sent out on Wintergrin—country-manipulation, and now a nice tidy little beheading. It's only wrong when we do it. When you do it, it is duty, honor, patriotism, prudence: You lose your liver and, alongside, you lose your brain. So Stalin has turned you into an executioner. Well, welcome to adulthood.

2

by **Romulus Linney**

Nuremberg, Germany - 1945-1946 - Counsel (56)

Counsel, an attorney, is being interviewed by Herman Goering, who needs a defense for his war crimes trial. Goering asks Counsel what he thinks of him. Counsel answers.

COUNSEL: I was fifty-six years old when you came to power. I watched my country—led by Hitler and by you—become one with itself, strong and vigorous. When you stood up—in those childish uniforms, with all those gleaming medals, dancing over a belly getting bigger and bigger every day—you made no bones about any of it. We were dazzled by Hitler, but we loved you. You were human, sometimes harsh but good at heart. A mirror for Germans. When you laughed, so did we. Then, with our cities in flames, we still loved you. I didn't know why, but we did. I still do. I will defend you with all my heart but I will never know what to call you.

INFINITY'S HOUSE
by Ellen McLaughlin
Humboldt Desert - 1850 - Fraulein Mittel (30's)

Here, a German pioneer woman who is dying of cholera speaks
to a kind stranger.

FRAULEIN MITTEL: You're the first man who's ever touched
me. More than to give me some work to do. I think that's what
I've always wanted most of all. To be touched.
[DOOLIN: She must have got out. She's loose. Christ, Annie.
(HE runs out)]
FRAULEIN MITTEL: And I thank you for that. At least that.
The sky is so heavy here, so bright and heavy. *(SHE lifts her arms
to the sky and drops them)* Hilda told me about husbands. Said they
lay on top of you and you think they'll crush you but they don't.
She says you think your ribs will crack they're so heavy. Like
bears. She said the weight of husbands was enormous. Like the
roof falling in. But that you'd be surprised. "You can hold them
up," she said, "we're stronger than we think we are." And I thought
I'd have a garden in America. I thought nothing could be harder
than mill work. I thought I'd never be lonely again. There would
be a man—he'd marry me—and at night in America he would come
to me, a man with a beard, and he would lay down upon me and
warm me and I could stand it. I would be strong enough in
America. *(SHE holds her arms up again)* I can stand it. Lay on
me. Let the roof fall in. I can hold you up. *(Her arms fall slowly.
SHE dies)*

CEMENTVILLE
by Jane Martin

Tennessee - Present - Mother (50's)

Bigman, a wrestling promoter, has hired Mother's two
daughters, called the Knockout Sisters, for his wrestling card.
When Mother arrives and sees Bigman's "stable," she addresses
them and Bigman.

MOTHER: Pretty run-down lookin' bunch.

[BIGMAN: Yeah, but wait 'til you see 'em in action!]

MOTHER: Y'all are dead meat. You're a two-bit tour playin'
morgue dates and you got never-was, never-will-be talent on the way
down. I wouldn't be caught dead puttin' my top attraction down this
pisshole but I got me a public relations problem. See, we messed
up, got ourselves into politics, put a crimp in our image. Now we
got to lay low, stay in shape an make a few bucks. On the upside
we probably goin' to get a film deal out of that mess, we're
negotiatin'. The Knockout Sisters is A-One, U.S. prime horseflesh.
While we're slummin' with you girls, you're going to have ace
crowds an make the only decent money you ever made in your
miserable lives. While we're together your sports pimp here...

(Indicating Bigman)

...gets me coffee. You understand? I say fuck a sheep, he fucks a
sheep, is that clear?

[BIGMAN: *(A big smile)* She got a great sense of humor, doesn't
she?]

MOTHER: Now think this over. How do you think a couple small-
town girls became the fourth biggest wrestling attraction in the
United States of America in two years?

(She pauses)

That's right. Mobbed up. Just like Sinatra. You capice? Now this
wrestlin' wears out an attraction, which is why we seque into film.
But meanwhile, meanwhile don't bruise the meat. You understand
me? You injure, deface or otherwise crumb up the dollar value on
my attraction you're going to hear some fucking Sicilian. Got it?
Dottie, Dolly, get in here.

THE DEATH OF ZUKASKY
by Richard Strand
Chicago - Present - Henry Marlino (40's)

Marlino's sales manager has just died. Marlino calls the sales
staff together for a meeting. He begins with an "inspiring"
anecdote.

MARLINO: You know, last night I went to see the Chinese
Acrobats. I was particularly struck by this one act they did. There
was a platform, maybe four feet high, and one of the Chinamen is
standing on that platform.   Then another Chinaman brings him a
chair and four champagne bottles. So he takes the chair, puts it on
top of the champagne bottles and then he does a handstand on top of
the chair which is on top of the bottles which is on top of the
platform. A handstand!
(Everyone tries to murmur impressed sounds.)
So okay, it doesn't sound like much so far. I couldn't do it, but
still, I shelled out twenty-two fifty and I need to see a little better
than that. But this little Chinaguy is just getting started. Because
they bring him a second chair. And he sets that second chair on top
of the first chair—upside down, you understand, so the legs are
pointing up at the ceiling—and pulls himself up into a handstand
again. Are you picturing this?
[BARRY: Uh…]
MARLINO: He's doing a handstand on top of a chair which is on
top of a chair which is on top of four champagne bottles which are
on top of a platform which is already four feet off the ground. And
I think, pretty good. I don't know that it's worth twenty-two fifty,
but it's pretty damn good anyway. I figured that was it. And then
they bring him *another* chair. Three chairs. They got three chairs
stacked on top of each other—balanced on champagne bottles—and
on top they got a Chinaman doing a handstand.   Now that's
amazing. That's goddamned amazing, don't you think?
[BARRY: Uh…]

THE DEATH OF ZUKASKY

MARLINO: But then they bring him *another* chair. And I'm thinking, it's impossible. No way is this guy making four chairs. But he keeps going. He makes four chairs. And five chairs. Five chairs!

(BARRY whistles.)

He's almost touching the ceiling. They can't reach him from the ground anymore—they're handing him chairs on the ends of poles. And this crazy Chinaman ends up stacking *six goddamned chairs on top of four champagne bottles on top of a four foot platform and he's on the top doing a handstand!* I can't figure how he's doing it. Looks like he ought to fall, but he doesn't. And then—*then*—he takes the top chair and tips it on an angle so that only the back two legs are touching the seat of the chair beneath it and *then* he kicks up into a handstand again. *Then he goes on one hand!*

[BARRY: One hand!]

MARLINO: *Every time I think he's done as much as he can do, he does something more!*

(MARLINO pauses and makes sure everyone is listening, which they are. Then he repeats, quietly, but with emphasis...)

Every time I think he's done as much as he can do, he does something more.

NIGHT-SIDE
by Shem Bitterman
Boston - Present - S (40's)

S is a woman who lives in a lonely world, alternating lives, mostly in her fantasies. Here, she enters into an escapist fantasy.

S: There's a plane leaving at eleven fifty to Santiago...

A red eye...

The young man behind the counter assures me that Santiago is exactly where I want to be.

He tells me of a lovely hotel there, where he has already booked an exquisite suite, and of the beaches I can explore, and the mountains.

He says it's all right there, in Santiago...all of it.

I am in awe...beaches, mountains, city all together...

What have I been doing with my life?

The fun of this adventure is coming together now.

And wasn't I lucky because the plane flies direct only twice a week, and one of the days just happens to be Friday...It's all too good to be true, like a sign from above, I was meant to travel tonight to Santiago...and he takes my credit card, and offers me a cookie, and I feel for a moment like I am at the dentist's office and before you know it I have the ticket in my hand and it's ten thirty eight only twelve and a half hours to kill before I am away from all this forever in Santiago...

...and over lunch at La Chateau I find myself so enthralled with the name Santiago, that it suddenly seems to me that Santiago and I were meant for one another, and gradually through the lunch, sweetened with a bottle of Chateau Vandome, I find that thought of returning to Boston impossible...In Santiago isn't it summer all year round, and don't they have lovely hyacinths and azaleas...Why surely there must be room for one more small flower shop in Santiago...

Yes, I can see it now...

The Spanish squares, wide and broad, and the policemen dressed in

71

NIGHT-SIDE

white...
No-one will mind if I try quietly to fit in there...
And I'll never have to watch Casey with her husband in Fort Worth
have her heart slowly broken...or think my hands long, boney
tendrils...or wish myself disappeared...
All that will be over with.

OUT THE WINDOW
by Neal Bell
New York City - Present - Jake (20's)

Jake, a parapalegic, wakes up in the morning very hung over.

JAKE: *(eyes closed)* WHO'S THERE? *(He reacts to his shout:)* Owww! Jeez Louise, whoever it was left a ten-inch surgical spike in my skull, you can have it back, let me try that again, little softer: Who's there? Andy?

(He feels the surrounding air with his hands.)

Nothing. Me and my chair...

(Far off a cock crows.)

I'd open my eyes but I'm guessing that light would not be what the doctor ordered, and speaking of tongue and spirit depressors... One of my sweat-socks snaked right up my leg, sometime in the night I think this was, and passed away in my mouth, could you bring me a glass of water, see if I can just flush the sucker, yo, Andrea, hey, little help...

(Again the off-stage rooster crows. Jake winces.)

And could somebody kindly get the hook for that bird?

(The rooster crows.)

Do I live on a farm? Survey SAYS... No. I don't live on a farm. OK, did I go to a party so trendy that animal acts were a part of the entertainment? Survey SAYS... I don't remember. Much about that party. At all. I recall a taxi-ride through the Park. And then a mahogany elevator. And then a lot of Republicans. People who

OUT THE WINDOW

looked like Republicans, anyway, bow-ties flapping away...and then you wheeling me out of the madding crowd, and into the dark and onto your bed, *somebody's* bed, whosever bed the party was, and the rest is the kind of history you're condemned to repeat...which I wouldn't mind, repeating, except next time, Andrea, sweetie, baby, doll, I'd like to remember. The way you feel. The way you taste. The way you move. For both of us. Remember all that, and not black out and be shovelled back into my chair, like a sack of sheep-dip, and shoved out into the hall or wherever I am, stark raving alone, if I *am* alone, if I open my eyes...if I open my eyes and you've slunk away—Andrea?... I'm going to feel, fair warning here, very crippled up and very done in by Life, as I know it now, and extremely very sorry I ever was born, it is going to get *that* ugly and whiny and borderline-truly-obnoxious, I swear, so be it on your delectable head, if I open my eyes...

(He opens his eyes.)

Andrea?

(He looks around.)

So you slopped me back in my chair after all, and abandoned me halfway up the kitchen...wall...

(He looks down, suddenly realizing his chair is up in the air, on a table.)

...and screw a Mallard. I'm up on a table. *(pause)* Screw a green and yellow Mallard sideways. How'd I...like a giant entree, defrosting. How'd I get up on a table?

OUT THE WINDOW
by Neal Bell
New York City - Present - Andy (20's)

Here, Andy tells her boyfriend, Jake, how she felt after his accident.

ANDY: I had to hope you wouldn't die. And then I had to hope there was still a mind, in this body that hadn't died, and couldn't move. And then, when the mind came back, I had to hope it wasn't buried alive in a body that only lay there, month after month. And then when the body moved at all, the tip of one finger, a twitch, I had to hope it would move again. And that more would move. That your fingers could hold a pencil someday. That your sphincter muscles could hold your piss. That your penis could hold a boner. That you could hold me. So I could love your body. And come. Then I had to hope you could come too.

PERMISSIONS ACKNOWLEDGMENTS

should be addressed to Robert A. Freedman Dramatic Agency, Inc., 1501 Broadway, Suite 2310, New York, NY 10036.

EXTREMITIES by William Mastrosimone. Copyright ©, 1978, 1984, by William Mastrosimone; "The Making of Extremities" Copyright ©, 1985, by William Mastrosimone. Reprinted by permission of the author's agent, George Lane, William Morris Agency, 1350 Avenue of the Americas, New York, NY 10019.

MY SISTER IN THIS HOUSE by Wendy Kesselman. Copyright ©, 1980, 1982, 1988, by Wendy Kesselman. Reprinted by permission of the author's agent, Lucy Kroll Agency, 390 West End Avenue, New York, NY 10024.

Excerpt from CLARA'S PLAY by John Olive. Copyright ©, 1982, 1984, by John Olive. This excerpt is reprinted by permission of the author and Samuel French, Inc. The use of it must be confined to study and reference. Attention is called to the fact that this excerpt, being duly copyrighted, may not be publicly read or performed or otherwise used without the permission of the author. All inquiries should be addressed to Samuel French, Inc. for stock and amateur use. All other rights inquiries should be addressed to Susan Schulman, A Literary Agency, 454 West 44th Street, New York, NY 10036.

A DIFFERENT MOON by Ara Watson. © Copyright, 1983, by Ara Watson. CAUTION: A DIFFERENT MOON, being duly copyrighted, is subject to a royalty. The stock and amateur production rights are controlled exclusively by the Dramatists Play Service, Inc., 440 Park Avenue South, New York, NY 10016. No stock or amateur performance of the play may be given without obtaining in advance, the written permission of the Dramatists Play Service, Inc., and paying the requisite fee. All inquiries concerning rights (other than stock and amateur rights) should be addressed to Bret Adams Limited, 448 West 44th Street, New York, NY 10036.

FULL HOOKUP by Conrad Bishop and Elizabeth Fuller. © Copyright, 1986, by Conrad Bishop and Elizabeth Fuller; © Copyright, 1982, by Conrad Bishop and Elizabeth Fuller as an unpublished dramatic composition. CAUTION: FULL HOOKUP, being duly copyrighted, is subject to a royalty. The stock and amateur production rights are controlled exclusively by the Dramatists Play Service, Inc., 440 Park Avenue South, New York, NY 10016. No stock or amateur performance of the play may be given without obtaining in advance, the written permission of the Dramatists Play Service, Inc., and paying the requisite fee. All inquiries concerning rights (other than stock and amateur rights) should be addressed to Lucy Kroll Agency, 390 West End Avenue, New York, NY 10024.

BARTOK AS DOG by Patrick Tovatt. © Copyright, 1983, by Patrick Tovatt. CAUTION: BARTOK AS DOG, being duly copyrighted, is subject to a royalty. The stock and amateur production rights are controlled exclusively by the Dramatists Play Service, Inc., 440 Park Avenue South, New York, NY 10016. No stock or amateur performance of the play may be given without obtaining in advance, the written permission of the Dramatists Play

77

PERMISSIONS ACKNOWLEDGMENTS

Mann.   Reprinted by permission of the author's agent, George Lane, William Morris Agency, 1350 Avenue of the Americas, New York, NY 10019.

HUSBANDRY by Patrick Tovatt. Copyright ©, 1983, 1984, by Patrick Tovatt. Reprinted by permission of the author's agent, Mary Harden, Bret Adams Limited, 448 West 44th Street, New York, NY 10036.

LEMONS by Kent Broadhurst. © Copyright, 1984, by Kent Broadhurst. CAUTION: LEMONS, being duly copyrighted, is subject to a royalty. The stock and amateur production rights are controlled exclusively by the Dramatists Play Service, Inc., 440 Park Avenue South, New York, NY 10016. No stock or amateur performance of the play may be given without obtaining in advance, the written permission of the Dramatists Play Service, Inc., and paying the requisite fee. All inquiries concerning rights (other than stock and amateur rights) should be addressed to Samuel Liff, c/o William Morris Agency, 1350 Avenue of the Americas, New York, NY 10019.

THE OCTETTE BRIDGE CLUB by P.J. Barry. Copyright ©, 1979, 1985, by P.J. Barry. Reprinted by permission of the author's agent, Samuel Liff, William Morris Agency, 1350 Avenue of the Americas, New York, NY 10019.

THE ROOT OF CHAOS by Douglas Soderberg. © Copyright, 1986, by Douglas Soderberg. CAUTION: THE ROOT OF CHAOS, being duly copyrighted, is subject to a royalty. The stock and amateur production rights are controlled exclusively by the Dramatists Play Service, Inc., 440 Park Avenue South, New York, NY 10016. No stock or amateur performance of the play may be given without obtaining in advance, the written permission of the Dramatists Play Service, Inc., and paying the requisite fee. All inquiries concerning rights (other than stock and amateur rights) should be addressed to Bret Adams Limited, 448 West 44th Street, New York, NY 10036.

THE AMERICAN CENTURY by Murphy Guyer. © Copyright, 1985, by Murphy Guyer. CAUTION: THE AMERICAN CENTURY, being duly copyrighted, is subject to a royalty. The stock and amateur production rights are controlled exclusively by the Dramatists Play Service, Inc., 440 Park Avenue South, New York, NY 10016. No stock or amateur performance of the play may be given without obtaining in advance, the written permission of the Dramatists Play Service, Inc., and paying the requisite fee. All inquiries concerning rights (other than stock and amateur rights) should be addressed to Bret Adams Limited, 448 West 44th Street, New York, NY 10036.

TWO MASTERS by Frank Manley. Copyright ©, 1985, by Frank Manley. Reprinted by permission of the author's agent, Peter Franklin, William Morris Agency, 1350 Avenue of the Americas, New York, NY 10019.

Excerpt from "21A" by Kevin Kling. Copyright ©, 1986, by Kevin Kling. This excerpt is reprinted by permission of the author and Samuel French, Inc. The use of it must be confined to study and reference. Attention is called to the fact that this excerpt, being duly

79